T0064492

Discovering the Inner You

VALERIE EDWARDS

BALBOA.PRESS

A DIVISION OF HAY HOUSE

Balboa Press books may be ordered through booksellers or by contacting:

Balboa Press
A Division of Hay House
1663 Liberty Drive
Bloomington, IN 47403
www.balboapress.com.au
AU TFN: 1 800 844 925 (Toll Free inside Australia)
AU Local: 0283 107 086 (+61 2 8310 7086 from outside Australia)

Print information available on the last page.

ISBN: 978-1-5043-2204-1 (sc)
ISBN: 978-1-5043-2224-9 (e)

Balboa Press rev. date: 09/26/2020

I dedicate this book to Irenee Stanton who has guided my spiritual development to the stage that has enabled me to write this book, through my guide Red Eagle. I have been sitting in a closed circle with Irenee for the past four years. Red Eagle came to me after about nine months of sitting.

The process was a gentle one. He first started to speak through me to the group. After a while he gave me inspirational poems, then teachings all leading up to the writing of this book.

Let me tell you, it has been a truly magical experience. Not all easy going as I had a lot of emotional stress to work through. But the longer I sat, the easier it became and the closer I got to my guide, Red Eagle, and my higher self. My life has been transformed. I am now full of love for myself and every extension of myself. Life is getting better day by day.

Thank you Irenee for your patience and dedication to your work for spirit.

God bless you.

Valerie Edwards

Contents

The Power Of Love

The power of love
Is what holds the key
The power of love
Will set each one free

Love is the essence
The very core
It is what each one
Is living for

Love for ourselves
Is where it must start
It must grow from within
Then flow through the heart

The stronger the love
For ourselves that we feel
The more love we have
To give others too

This love must be pure
With no strings attached
For what we give out
We should never want back

For this way love
Will be free to grow
An expanding circle
Free to flow
This circle it widens
With every spin
For what we give out
Will return again

Return with a strength
That has multiplied
Doubled, then tripled
Growing stronger and wider
With each new tide

Now if we swim
Against this tide
We will grow week
Begin to feel sick inside

For just like a plant
Denied the sun and rain
It will never bloom again
Its leaves will curl
It will wither and die
Not knowing the beauty
It had
Kept hidden inside

When it could have bloomed
Grown into a tree
Its branches spreading
For the world to see
Its flowers
Its perfume
Filling the air
A thing of splendour
For all to share
Giving freely of itself
Creating our air

Now we could grow
Just like this tree
A thing of splendour
For the world to see
An example of how God
Meant for us to be

Just like the tree
We need sun and rain
To bath in the light
Feel its warmth again
Nourish ourselves
With love for our soul
For far too long
It has been kept in the cold
Denied, ignored
Unworthy of love

We live on the surface
What the mirror reveals
Is only a covering
A thin veneer
We become paranoid
We are too fat
Too thin
And what is this lump
That has appeared on our chin

Now we know
We will never fit in
Our self esteem
Has grown quite dim

If there were no mirrors
We would not know
How we looked
It would not trouble us so
No magazines
No T.V. shows
Saying
This is the way
You should look you know
Your hair's all wrong
The colour of your skin
Your eyes are to small
Or bulging

There is a difference
Between vanity and love
This is what we are speaking of
Vanity is seen with the eyes
Love is felt with the heart

So next time you feel
You don't measure up
Go within
Fill your cup
With love for your Soul
It will shine through
The world will see
A beautiful new you

The Journey

When we set out on a journey, we usually take a collection of things we think we will need to complete the journey safely. It may include things like a road map, a compass, a return ticket.

But when we take an inner journey, we have no such tools to guide us.

There are no road maps, no compass, no return tickets to be found.

On this inner journey we have only faith, so we need to slip into this journey slowly, a little at a time. There is no great rush. We are not competing with anyone or anything. It is a journey of our own choice, our own making.

So, how do we begin this journey? What are our first steps going to be? How can we judge what progress, if any, we are making? Will there be any sign posts along the way?

I am writing this book to guide you, as a sign post you can look to. It will not give you all the answers as no two inner journeys are the same. Besides, if I were to give you all the answers to your questions, what would be the point of your journey. What would you discover about yourself, your own truths, if you already believed in mine? Believe me when I tell you no two truths are the same. We are all on different pathways although they all lead to the one place.

I want this to be a joyous experience for you, one that will enrich your life, transform your soul.

CHAPTER ONE

Let the journey begin

F ind yourself a quite spot where you feel comfortable, at ease with yourself and your surroundings. Put up a do not disturb sign, take the phone off the hook, slip into your most comfortable clothes and relax. Try and make it the same time each day, beginning with just five or ten minutes. Do not pressure yourself into sitting for any longer. Do not think of anything in particular, just close your eyes and let your thoughts slip by. Listen to your favourite music if it helps to calm you. Have a clock where you can look straight at it when you open your eyes. This way you will not be constantly thinking what time is it. Just glance up now and again to reassure yourself.

Once you have gotten into the routine of sitting, you will be much more relaxed. Remember you have nothing to prove, no deadlines to meet. No trains, boats or planes to catch. This is a journey of discovery with no set timetable.

The further you go into your journey the more you will discover about yourself. You will grow in confidence and strength, inner strength. The love you feel for yourself and those around you will intensify.

I am not saying it will be all smooth sailing. There will be times when you become very frustrated and annoyed with yourself and the whole process. You will at times think you are going nowhere, feel like a fool and a fraud. At times you may even stop, say to yourself, "I have had enough'. This is just plain nonsense, but after a while if you truly want to grow, to evolve you will be back sitting, waiting, watching and listening. Yes listening. Listening to that little inner voice whispering in your ear, booming up from the depth of your soul. Or maybe it is not a voice at all. Maybe it is just a thought. A thought that you have no idea of, no answer to. Where did it come from? What does it mean? Follow that thought, write it down, ponder on it ask for more thoughts to come.

Now let us not lose sight of what this journey is all about. It is not about becoming psychic, reading minds, cards or other paraphernalia. It is about discovering the inner you. The "you", you hide from the outside world by putting on many different fronts, and disguises.

It is about finding out who the soul behind your eyes really is. Where she has been, what inner most secrets she can reveal to you? How she can help you to develop and grow emotionally and spiritually in this lifetime. This journey will take you over serene valley's, rocky mountains, to the very depth of the deepest ocean. It will take you to the highest mountain top where your heart will soar.

We have talked at length about what we can expect to achieve on our inner journey, about the feelings of elation and frustration. Now let us take a look at the progress we can expect to make.

As with anything that is worthwhile, we get out of it what we are prepared to put into it. In other words the more time we invest in our inner journey the more rewards we will reap. The more committed we are to growing, the more we will grow.

If we set aside ten minutes a day, for let us say a month and stick to this, at the end of the month we could expect to see some progress. Even if it is just to the point of being able to settle – to let our thoughts drift by without really getting involved in them. This is a major breakthrough. Once we are able to achieve this, we are on our way.

If on the other hand, we have not been all that dedicated and have only set ten minutes aside every now and then, we cannot expect the same results. We would be very lucky after a month of on and off sitting to be even able to sit still for that length of time, without feeling some discomfort.

You must get into the routine of sitting. Think of it as an important appointment you have with a very special friend. A friend who can enhance your life, your world, your future. Try never to break the appointment, always be on time, do not make excuses . . . just do it.

Once you get into the routine and start to make progress it will automatically become an appointment you look forward too. You will find a friend whose company you really enjoy. Someone you can be completely honest with. You can be sure they will be completely honest with you, for truth comes with silence. Make no mistake of this fact. Truth, comes with silence.

> Sit in the silence
> Bask in its calm
> Lose yourself totally
> To its faithful charm
> Allow it to wash you
> Cleanse away pain
> Sweep out the shadows
> Make you whole again
> For silence is wisdom
> Weakness and strength
> It breaks down barriers
> Removes our defence
> We have built up around us
> With each tiny step

Of doubt and confusion
Fear and regret

Emotions that swamp us
We cover with noise
Aggravation yes anger
Will cover the cause
For we cannot face it
The silence, the pain
Of facing the truth
Once again
But until we face it
Conquer the fear
Doubt will rule
Forever here

CHAPTER TWO

Becoming committed

Now once we have decided that we wish to continue on our inner journey, that we are prepared to constantly put aside a set amount of time each day, that we are prepared to increase this time as we evolve to say fifteen minutes for the next month. Then we can expect to see the results in our every day life. We will begin to have more confidence in our own ability. Making decisions will become easier. Little things will not annoy us as they used to.

You really need to keep a diary and jot down any new or unusual experiences and feelings you have. It does not matter how trivial you may think they are at the time. They will act as signposts to your progression.

At the end of the second month, read through the diary. Take note of any changes in your life. Do not disregard them as coincidences. Compare how you feel now, to how you felt before starting to meditate. Are you a more positive person? Are your emotions more constant, less up and down? Be honest with your answers. Remember there is no pressure to perform, do not compare your development to anyone else's, as no two inner journeys are the same.

Look at the way you are sitting. Do you get restless after fifteen minutes? Do you feel you are ready and would benefit by increasing your sitting time to twenty minutes for the next month?

If the answer is no just continue on the way you are for the next month, then go over it again. Have I seen any improvement in the way I sit? Am I still restless watching the clock or can I now sit still and relaxed for the whole fifteen minutes? Does the time fly by or drag? Is my mind still preoccupied with the day's events or can I now push these aside to a point where the mind is still, in complete alignment with the body. We are aiming for the body, mind and Soul to merge into one. To feel at peace with ourselves and the universe.

> Peace, peace inner peace
> I never knew there could be such bliss
> No words can explain
> The elation I feel
> When I merge into one
>   With the Universe too
>
> I float on a cloud
> That is as light as a ray
> Of beautiful colours
> Encasing me today
> They merge into one
> With the beat of my heart
> Throbbing with colour
>   A crystal collage
>
> How can I tell you
> What my eyes can see
> No words can express
> What I hold close to me

As we grow in confidence we can experiment with different ways of sitting. We may wish to experience one of the many popular meditation tapes, or perhaps try meditating in the dark with a candle. Do not be afraid to try new methods once you have sitting under control. Remember the object of the exercise is to get a balance, a merging of body, mind and soul. To be at one with the universe.

There are many different ways of achieving this. We need to find the one that best suits us. The one that unlocks the key to other dimensions. Do not, I repeat, do not experiment with mind altering drugs. These will only lead to misery and pain. There are no short cuts to discovering the inner you. In fact, by taking mind altering drugs, you hide the inner you behind more illusions, more layers of false truths. Remember the further under the surface you have buried yourself, the longer it will take to dig yourself out.

Many people experience what I call ego trips. They fill themselves up with pills or booze and go into a stupor not a trance. From this stupor they hallucinate many weird and wonderful things. But, none of them are truths. By the very act of taking a drug of any kind they have denied themselves the very truth they claim to be seeking.

Or have we been fooling ourselves all along? Are we really not prepared to face up to our own reality? Are we still to infantile in our evolvement to handle who we really are?

When you feel you are completely ready to move on to the next step, the next phase of your development, do so. Do not attempt to sit any longer than twenty minutes until it feels completely safe and relaxed. I feel I cannot stress the point to much. There is no great rush. It is not a competition. No one is judging you other than yourself. If you feel comfortable at the ten-minute level for twelve months, two years, what does it matter. The only thing that really matters is that you are relaxed and at ease in your own company. That you feel safe and loved.

Valerie Edwards

I look to the sunset
The redness of hue
These subtle colours
Stir memories anew

I sit in the twilight
And ponder the cause
Of elation I'm feeling
There must be a cause

Or is it a memory
Buried deep inside
I can no longer suppress
No longer hide
Whatever the answer
Whatever the key
I know I will find it
Inside of me

It's a longing I'm feeling
The will to be free
Of these restrictions
Encompassing me

In the darkness I wallow
Seeking the light
searching the shadows
of my mind

I need to be still now
Let my thoughts fly
Like clouds on a wind shift
Scattering by

Do not try to catch them
Let them fly free
To what destination
Is a mystery to me

I must gather my courage
Calm myself down
Plant my feet firmly
On the ground
Let my heart guide me
Show me the way
To light my path clearly
In its golden ray

Hope springs eternal
If only we knew
That deep down inside us
An oriole grew

A bird of such wisdom
Beauty and power
Of such adoration
For this sacred flower

At times I might wither
Wilt with despair
But the love of my oriole
Carries me through

CHAPTER THREE

Let us now talk of love

L ove is the strongest emotion felt by mankind. It is the opposite to hate. Hate is simply love kept in the dark. Yes, the dark side of love. Think about this. We take all the beautiful aspects of love and turn them inside out. Instead of using love as a tool to heal ourselves, we use it as a weapon to turn on ourselves, to destroy ourselves and those who come in connect with us. Instead of letting love flow we supress it. Bottle it up. Dam it inside ourselves until we can no longer contain it. It explodes into anger, greed and jealousy. All these adverse emotions come seeping out of the cracks in our dam of emotions. We put plaster over these cracks by building another façade to hide behind. We bury these emotions deeply within us, hoping no one else will notice we are not perfect. That we are vulnerable to the opinions of others annoys us. It makes us feel less than we are, less than we are capable of being. Instead of looking at this, feeling this emotion, talking about it with our friends, our loved ones, we suppress it inside ourselves covering it with layers and layers of guilt.

What do I have to feel guilty about you may ask? Guilt is just another word that we use to express that we are unworthy. Unworthy of what? Unworthy of our very existence. We feel so inferior to the other perfect beings we see before us. They come across so sure of what they are doing and why they are doing it. They seem to be so utterly in control of their lives.

They do not worry what others are thinking. They know all the answers. They are so strong where we are so weak. They express themselves so beautifully with such intellect and charm. They make us feel less than perfect, indeed they make us feel so inferior, so tiny, so weak. They seem to suck the very breath of our existence from us. Why can we not be like them, perfect.

However, if you were to study one of these role models, day by day, night by night, if you could really see inside their brain, their Soul, you would discover they are just the same as you, hiding behind an illusion, a façade. All their bravado is just an act. Or is it perhaps their ego.

Let us look at the life we are living
Let us analyse
The very many treasures
We have kept hidden inside
Hidden by an illusion
A façade we hide behind
To protect us from each other
So we may come across
Brave and strong

We hide our mixed emotions
For fear of looking week
For fear of being exposed
From the illusion that we seek
To build up around us
To hide the very things
That make us very special
Although we think
They make us weak

We must try to understand
That the weak
Are sometimes strong
For it takes great courage
To admit that we are wrong
To stand up and be counted
To turn the other cheek
To admit we are only human
That beauty is skin deep
If we wash away the make-up
If we peel away the skin
If we penetrate the heart
What will we find within

Just a lonely Soul
Just a simple friend
Who really is quite special
If they let the sunlight in
Underneath the covering
Behind the steel façade
We all are just Gods children
As numerous as the stars
For there are many galaxies
Many forms of life
That we will soon discover
When the time is right

So let's wash off the make-up
Let's peel away the skin
Let's penetrate the heart
Reveal what lies within
For how will we manage
To hide our many fears
When we are all stripped naked
When the son of God appears

I know it's very scary
I know it's hard
To know where to start
With all these mixed emotions
We think come from the heart
But they are really our ego
Just trying to hem us in
Trying to keep us prisoner
Locked away from the truth
We hold within

So let us not surrender
Let us all stand tall
Take away the barriers
Let the tear drops fall
Surrender to our emotions
Admit that we are weak
That we know not all the answers
But that we are willing to seek

The truth that has been hidden
Buried deep within
That we are part of God
That our ego can't hem us in

That we are free to travel
To seek our higher self
On this journey of discovery
That we must take for ourselves

CHAPTER FOUR

How we create our reality

L et us now discuss the ego, that controlling little voice inside of our being. That innermost feeling that seems to get hurt at the slightest form of rejection. The ego is what makes us swell up with pride at a job well done. It is also what makes our eyes green with envy at the success of someone who has succeeded in an area where we have failed.

There are many different facades we hide behind. Many different disguises, many forms of protection we encase ourselves in. But the ego is the most harmful one of all. The ego can fill our minds with so much poison, can make us feel so superior to our fellow peers. If we let our ego have complete control we can very easily slip out of our depth, get lost in a world of insecurity. We begin to live a lie, we become so paranoid we no longer know what our true strengths and weaknesses are. We become so lost in our own world of fantasy, in trying to impress others, we tell bigger and bigger lies. Believe me there is no one more boring, or self-deceiving, then a soul on an ego trip.

How can we avoid turning into one of these souls of self-delusion? By being completely honest with ourselves. By saying each time we catch ourselves exaggerating, stretching the truth. Why did I do that? What need do I have inside of me that is crying out for help? Make no mistake, it is a cry for help. Look at me I am worthy of your attention, of your love. I am not some inferior being to be suppressed, ignored, denied. God I am within, I am. Acknowledge me, love me.

Does this take you by surprise? Does this shock you? That I should dare call myself a God. That I dare to suggest that you should think of yourself as a God. The truth of the matter is that simple. We are all part of the whole. Each and every thing you perceive before you is connected to you. Is an extension of you in a different form. We are all God expressing and creating in our own way. Creating our own reality, our own heaven or hell. We can become and do anything we wish to experience. I will go one step further than this and really make you think. All that you are, all that you ever will be, is controlled by your thought patterns. If your thoughts are very regimented and closed to new ideas, new concepts, you will remain a very regimented closed person for the simple fact that you are closing off your evolution pathway. How can you expect to evolve if you have closed yourself down to this channel – this opening to the inner you.

All thoughts come from within. All expression comes from within. All growth comes from within. So if you stop this flow, if you dam up the spring of information, you will stagnate in your own arrogance, your own self-denial. Do you understand what I am trying to convey to you? What you are feeling, what you are experiencing is of your own making, your own set of circumstances. You are what you want to be at this present moment, at this point in time. You are the maker of your dreams, the creator of your fortunes. Whether they be good or bad. Heaven or hell, you created it, you dreamed it, you thought it. Do you understand? It is so simple, yet it seems to be the hardest thing to comprehend. You create your reality with your thought patterns. Remember what you are thinking in this moment sets up what will be happening in the next and the next and the next and so it goes. It is that simple.

Now you may begin to have some idea of just how important your inner journey really is. Of how important it is to be completely honest with yourself, to love yourself and to nourish the God you are within. Do not deny that God. Do not supress him, bury him under layers and layers of false images, facades, illusions, trying to make yourself perfect. Because believe me, the real you, the one buried deep within, the one you sometimes get a glimpse of in the bathroom mirror is just that, perfect, if you would only let them be. If you would only trust them, allow them to surface and lead you on a path of discovery. A path of evolution. I am giving you the key, the ticket to this wonderful journey. It is love of yourself and all that you are. Remember, remember the things that you dislike about yourself. To use a stronger word the things that you hate about yourself. These are the things that you really need to work on. You really need to analyse these points, ponder on them at length. Where did this dislike spring from, what was its origin? Was it in this lifetime or has it carried over from a past life?

There are many ways of doing this. Some work better then others. Some suit the individual better than others. But I will tell you of one sure way that will work for all. It really is foolproof but you must stick to it. As we said before, we only get out of anything what we are prepared to put into it. You must give one hundred percent. You must go all the way or not at all. It is that simple.

Take a piece of paper, write down the first thought that comes to mind. It can be anything, it does not have to be related to anything in particular. Write down this thought and ponder on it. Think about how it relates to the things you hate most about yourself. Now, it is very important that you are honest with yourself and sometimes being honest with ourselves is very difficult. Sometimes we buried our own true feelings so deep that we really have no idea how to be honest with ourselves. We really do not know what truth is. If that is the case with you, do not despair. Just trust the strongest instinct. It usually is the first thing that comes to mind.

It is the God within trying to reach you, trying to help you. Let us not forget who we are ever again. Let us draw on the power within to create a world that is beautiful, joyous, and full of love. Love for every part of us, every extension of us. Then and only then will we be free to travel to other dimensions without the restrictions we place upon ourselves. Without a doubt and fear overshadowing us, preventing us from being all that we can and should be. I am not saying that any of this will happen overnight. It will take time and patience, lots of patience. It is a slow process and as I have said before, we get out of it what we are prepared to put into it.

Once you have written down on a piece of paper and are happy that you are being honest with yourself, meditate on the thought and the way it relates to your present situation. Does it make you feel angry or happy? Does it stir up good thoughts or bad? Just keep meditating on this word until you feel perfectly at ease with every aspect of it. Then write down another word that springs to mind. Before writing down this next word, ask for help. I feel sure that by this stage your Guides will have made contact with you. They will be aware of the fact you are opening your mind, that you are now ready to move ahead with your evolution, your growth. They will now be very keen to help you in any way they can. Once you have asked for their help, write down the first word that comes to mind once again. Go over the same routine as with the last word. Keep doing this until you run out of words. It should keep you busy for quite some time.

Do not give up, just keep plodding away as it will help you

a great deal in many ways. If you can keep doing this, it will speed up your growth, your evolution. Think of it as a mind game, play it, enjoy it, have fun with it. It does not have to be strictly serious to work. The more you enjoy it, the more you will keep up with it, the more you will grow.

I am going to go in a completely different direction now. I want you to imagine the world as a tiny ball. A ball that has no beginning or end. Place yourself on this ball. It can be at the top of the ball, the middle, or any point that you feel comfortable. When you have chosen a place, pick a colour that makes you feel happy and secure. Wrap all your fears, your insecurities for the future in this colour and place them on the ball in your chosen position. Now spin that colour in your mind until it becomes the complete ball, until it vibrates to the frequency of this colour. Am I making sense to you? Do you understand that which I am trying to convey to you? Bring the colour and the ball into one. If you have chosen a purple colour to wrap your fears in and have placed them in the middle of the ball, you will end up with a purple ball pulsating to the vibration of purple. The aim of this exercise is to get all your emotions moving in the one direction pulsating at the same frequency. It may be hard at first to manage this as our fears come from many directions, many different areas of our lives. What we are trying to do here, trying to achieve, is to merge them into one. That way they do not seem so immense, so overpowering. We have drawn them all together into one small package. Do this meditation as often as you can until you have it down pat. Then once a week should keep your fears to a minimum.

Now let us take a close look at the word fear. What does it convey to you?

Does it convey darkness, a darkness so dense that you can no longer see your hand in front of you? This is what fear really is, not being able to see into the future, not knowing what is going to happen next. The unknown. That which we have never experienced before. Fear of failure, fear of pain, fear of being exposed, fear of being stripped naked of all our reserves. Fear of being seen for who we really are and not measuring up. Failure, shame, weakness, being made to feel small and insignificant. We can break it down even more. What is the thing you fear most? Exposure? Having to come out from your little hiding place and be exposed to all. Letting the world see you as you really are, warts and all, is pretty scary stuff is it not? The feeling we are not perfect, that we do not measure up to those we place above us, those we think really matter, those we wish to impress, can be very debilitating. Fear is all these things and more.

If we took all our fears and analysed them, if we placed them into perspective, they would not feel as immense as we imagined them to be. The trouble is we never drag them out into the light and look at them. Face them and they will lose their power over you. Try it. Pick out your worst fear on a bright sunny day. Pick it out and look at it from all angles. Why does fear have so much power over me? Where is it coming from? How can I free myself from it? What is the worst possible outcome arriving from this fear? Think of the worst possible thing that could happen and face it. Live it. Breath it in, immerse yourself in it. Conquer it and you will be free of it. Swirl it in your purple or green, yellow or blue ball. Get control over it. Do not let it have control over you any longer. Remember to do this on a warm sunny day in a place where you feel very safe and secure. Ask your guides for help and protection. Never do this when you are feeling vulnerable or down. Wait until you are feeling good about yourself and your progress. Once you have done this with one fear, move on to the next and the next and so on.

Once we have overcome our fears, we are well on our way to being our complete self. Our whole self in all its glory.

Connected to the sun, moon and stars. The very essence of our being will shine through. There will be no way of containing it, for you will just glow. It will be as if a light has been turned on when you walk into a room, you will radiate, you will shine. Your love for yourself and every extension of you will shine through, it is that simple. It really is. We can live in this world as an outsider looking on, or we can be part of it. The choice is yours and yours alone. Why live in fear of the truth when the truth can set you free. Imagine no more feelings of anger or resentment, doubt or fear. Just a feeling of complete bliss, of love and well-being. To know deep down that everything is going to turn out for the best at all times. A complete feeling of trust.

The further we travel on our inner journey, the more truths we will discover. We will find a whole new world opening up to us. A world of hope, for once we reach a point on our inner journey where we have complete trust in our guides, our teachers, there will be no room for negativity. We will see only the positive side of things, for we will know deep in our heart that no matter what happens, it is for the good of our higher self. That there is a lesson to learn, or emotion we need to experience. Because this is what living is all about. This is the whole point of our existence.

Learning, experiencing, growing, living. The more emotions we have experienced, the more a part of the whole we can become. We never really know the depth of the water if all we ever experience is the level of our big toe. Do you not see? We have to live through an experience, an emotion before we can grow from it. If Tom, Dick and Harry tell you about it, it is not the same as experiencing it for yourself. You still do not know for sure in your heart of hearts how deep the water is or how it feels against your skin. The coldness, the wetness, the exhilarating feeling of the water. When you have truly experienced it you can then say to yourself this is what Tom, Dick and Harry were talking about. This is what they felt. It was so exhilarating, so uplifting, I now know in my heart of hearts how deep the water is, how it feels on my skin. You can now relate your experience to a friend, but they will never truly grow until they have experienced it for themselves. Is this now clear to you? Do you understand the importance of experiencing for yourself?

This is the way of evolution. This is the way of growth. This is the whole point of being born into the physical form. To feel, to experience, to grow.

Love and light to you my dear ones.

CHAPTER FIVE

The way we live

We will begin the next chapter with a poem. It is a poem of love, a poem of growth. A poem of life.

I sit at the window and watch the rain
The crystal drops fog the window pane
They obscure my vision
They block my view

What is this thing I am looking too
I see the movement
I glimpse the form
Is it welcoming
Is it warm

Or is it a danger
My eyes cannot see
I prick my ears
I listen and wait
What is that noise
Is it the gate
Or is it my imagination
Just playing tricks

The rain is clearing
I wander outside

There is nothing to fear
I do not have to hide
For now I have faced it
Stilled my mind
Used my senses
Everything's fine

Trust in your instincts
Trust in your Guide
Believe that they
Are on your side
That they know better
Their vision is clear
They can see the big picture
From here

Their heart is pure
Their love is strong
Remember you can do no wrong
For it is all a lesson
In the school of life

Live it, enjoy it
Just let it flow
Moment by moment
Let yourself grow
Stretch out your branches
Stretch your brain
Realise that this is only a game

A game of life
Of expansion, or pain
For without pain
It would not be the same

For if we cannot taste it
The sea of despair
We will not appreciate
The beauty there
For behind every sadness
Behind every tear
We grow in compassion
We expand our view
Broaden our horizons
Look at life anew

In this chapter we will concentrate more on the way in which we live our lives. Do we live a very hurried life or a life of peace and calm? Do we get lots of sleep and exercise? Do we eat a healthy diet? All these things and more will have a bearing on your spiritual development and on reaching the inner you, the higher self.

So let us start with diet and work our way through from there. I cannot stress enough the importance of the food we place inside our bodies; we eat to give ourselves energy. Energy to create life, to create movement and growth. Without this energy our body would slow down. We would find it very difficult to maintain any form of lifestyle for too long. After a prolonged period without energy our bodies really start to break down. They begin to close themselves down to protect their vital organs. The organs that really keep everything running. So you can see even by this simple explanation how important a healthy diet really is.

This energy supply has to not only fuel the body, but the brain as well. The think tank needs lots of energy if it is to survive. But if we wish it to grow, to expand itself, it will need even more fuel, more energy. More food of the right kind. The living kind. That's right we should only eat food that is alive. Food that is pulsating with energy, with life. How can we expect to get energy from a dead thing. A thing whose life has left it. This kind of food will keep us alive but it will not allow sufficient energy for us to grow, to expand, to evolve. Does this make sense to you? If you wish to grow you need to fuel that growth with food that is alive with its own life force, its own energy. Let us look at alive foods, foods that are crisp and succulent. A fresh red apple is alive and pulsating with life force, with energy. A crisp head of lettuce, a crunchy carrot. All foods with lots of colour and crispness. These are growth foods. The brain foods, along with nuts and grains. The fresher the food the more of their life force will be passed on to us when we eat it. Do you see? What is the point of eating dead food, it will only clog up the body, organs and glands. It will build up a store of fats we would be better off without. Dead food is just that. Dead! So try to eat this food in only very small amounts. It would not be wise to over indulge in it often, especially before we meditate as the body has a very hard time disposing of the waste from these dead foods. So remember to eat only minute portions of them. The more brain food we eat the more we enhance our growth, our evolvement. Our body is constantly rebuilding itself, recreating itself. This takes a lot of energy so until we are capable of hooking up directly to universal energy, we need to eat a good supply of food pulsating with its own life force.

Let us now move on to exercise. Exercise is another very important growth factor. Do not under estimate the need for exercise. We need to keep the body alert. We do this by exercising, by moving the joints and muscles. This in turn gets the body fluids moving, it keeps the motor humming away in rhythm with the soul. There has to be a connection between body, mind and soul. They have to be in balance, to be in harmony, beating to the same drum so to speak. Do you understand? Exercise is the key here. It holds the key to balance. It does not need to be strenuous exercise but it must be constant, a little each day is what is needed. Yoga is a very good form of exercise. It is a very calming form; it stills the mind as it invigorates the body and nourishes the soul. But whatever form of exercise you choose it is important to do a little each day. Even if it is taking a long slow walk. It will get the body fluids moving creating balance in our body mind and Soul. So try to have a set time period where you exercise. Get into a routine of say twenty minutes a day to begin with, then try to increase to sixty minutes over a period of time. An hour a day will make a big difference to your life. Even if you were to do nothing else to add to your growth, an hour a day of gentle exercise would work wonders over a period of time. But if we add meditation and good diet to this, we are going to advance much quicker and we do want to advance, do we not? So, your routine for the day so far is to set aside a period of time for exercise, meditation and good diet.

Now let us move on to feeding the brain with good nourishing food. Food of another kind. Thoughts. The brain really needs a good diet of thought. Positive thought. These can be in the form of affirmations. This is another, important part of development. Affirmations are a group of words we say on a regular basis. They can be in any form so long as they are positive and make us feel good. Let us say we have no confidence in our ability to create. A good affirmation here would be to say each day – I am a very creative person, there is no limitation to my creativity. Whatever negative feeling you have about yourself, create a positive affirmation to conquer this feeling of inadequacy. Positive thought patterns make for positive lives. Positive affirmations break down barriers, build bridges. They act as a link, a trigger to deep rooted memories. They release us from the past and pave the way for future events in our lives.

How do we go about choosing these affirmations? Which one will work best for us? Once again, we need to find out what is really missing in our lives. What special need do we have inside of us crying out for help?

By now you should be well into your thought game. This should give you a good idea of what is missing in your life. What changes you would like to make, what areas you need to work on. Have a close look at your feelings and how you relate to different people and situations. What fears you still have remaining, what doubts come flooding in? What makes you feel happy? What makes you feel sad? Do you have confidence to tackle new things, to go places by yourself without worrying what people will think of you? It is all a matter of building confidence in yourself, of loving yourself, of knowing that you are worthy of the very best of everything. You need to feel good about yourself at all times, in all situations. Tall order you might say, but it is possible. Do you deserve anything less, are you worthy of less? I think not. Remember you are God. You are part of God, part of all that is. So anything less than the very best is just not good enough. You are a very precious soul on a journey of discovery, do not fight it, rejoice in it. Fly with it, throw yourself right in the deep end. Lose your fear of the unknown. Face it. Conquer it. Thrive on it. God bless you all.

I am the light within
The power, the flame
I am known by many names
I come to you in many forms
But what I truly am
Is love
Pure unconditional love
I surround you
I pulsate in you
Through you
I can and will
Conquer all
All you have to do is trust
Set yourself adrift
Allow yourself to flow
To create to grow
Do not smother yourself
In self-pity and despair
Rise up above this
Fly high with the Eagles
Catch the updraught
That leads to other dimensions
Other galaxies
They are waiting, watching
Set yourself free
Like a leaf adrift
On the wind
You will never regret it
I promise you

CHAPTER SIX

Living in the moment

Now we come to living in the moment. From the time we are very young children we are taught to look to the future for things of pleasure or pain. Christmas is a good example of this. If you're a good boy Johnny, Santa will bring you a new bike or if Suzie eats all her dinner up, she will get a Barbie doll. They are not taught to enjoy the now moment. It is always some moment in the future when they will find happiness. At the moment they are just filling in time, trying to make it pass as quickly as possible until a birthday or Christmas.

Or we can look at it from another point of view. Many parents instil fear into their little children. Fear of the future. If you are not a good boy Johnny, Santa will not bring you that bike. He is watching you. So little Johnny is ever fearful or doing the wrong thing. He cannot relax and enjoy living in the now for fear of the future. What a way to bring up children. We are making them paranoid from such an early age it is no wonder that as adults we have such hang ups. Little Johnny and Suzie would have been quite happy living in the now moment creating a very happy uncomplicated life for themselves. They would never have dreamed of a Santa who rewarded them if they were good. They most definitely would not have dreamt up a Santa who would deny them if they did not do as the adults told them to do. After all they are creating their own reality, growing, learning by experiencing.

We all know there must be a set of rules if society is going to live in harmony. But these rules should never be built on fear. Do you not agree? Can you not see the reasons for this? Fear is a very negative force. A force that instils all that is darkness into the minds of children. It then shows up in teenagers as anger and confusion. They lose sight of what life is all about. They have lost love of themselves. All because of fear. All because of threats and restrictions on their ability to create. To live in the now moment.

The now moment is a very precious gift that should never be taken lightly. It should never be taken for granted. We should live it to the fullest. Each and every moment should be used to express, to grow, to awaken the inner glow. The feeling of elation when we are at peace with ourselves and the universe. What is the point of living for tomorrow for it may never come, it may never materialise. It can be swept away from us in a blink of an eye and what will we have to show for it. Material possessions. What good are they to us when we no longer live in the physical form.

What I am trying to say to you my dear ones is do not throw this life away. Enjoy it, immerse yourself in it. Use it to grow and develop, to experience. Experience joy, pain, fear, anger, all these emotions and more. Experiencing is living life to the fullest, no matter what the stage of your development. Cherish each step, wallow in the emotion. Soak up every drop of it.

Have no regrets. Do not look to the past with sorrow. Do not lament for things gone by. For we cannot go back to yesterday and tomorrow seems so far away. So live for the here and now. Look back to the past if you must but do so with joy, with elation for all the things you have experienced that have made you the person you are today. Think of how far you have come in terms of development, growth and in discovering the inner you. Just think how much you knew when you turned the first page and how much you know now. Look at everything that happens to you as growth. Look forward to the many twists and turns your life is taking, embrace them to you. Do no bemoan, "why me" just except them and move on with your life, your adventure, your journey. Do you not see, as we have said before life is a journey of discovery. It is a thrilling adventure and as in any exciting book we would sometimes like to skip the pages when the suspense is too much and go directly to the end to see what happens.

Unfortunately in our book of life this is not possible as we all have free will and the story line is likely to change at any time with very little notice. We will end up at the same destination but we may take an entirely different route. So you can see it is very hard to say exactly what is going to happen next week, let alone next year.

Living in the now moment is another very important step in discovering the inner you. Put it to practise, live it and watch your life change for the better.

Rise up, rise up
To greet the dawn
Rise up, rise up
To a brand-new morn
The birds are singing
Greeting the sun
With mother nature
They are as one
They live each moment as it comes
They have no safety net
No credit card
No nest egg for the future
At home in a jar
They do not need this
For they already know
Deep in their heart
God loves them so
He will not abandon
Cease to hear the cry
Of lifting emotion
Echoing by
Filling the morning
With music so sweet
Making each moment
So wonderfully complete
So live it, embrace it
Drown in its power
Beat your own drum
Hour after hour
Moment by moment
Materialise
Things of great beauty
Before your eyes
Restore a balance

A place in your heart
Of trust and devotion
For this sacred flower
Allow it to open
The petals to bloom
Send out the perfume
Across the room
To build a new moment
To follow the last
A moment of beauty
Of power of joy
Of living, creating
An uplifting world
A world of completeness
A garden to grow
Things of great beauty
For God loves you so

CHAPTER SEVEN

Feelings of the heart

Have you ever wondered where these feelings, deep in your heart spring from? Have you ever asked yourself why do I feel so deeply in my heart? The pain, the joy, the love becomes a physical thing we can actually feel in our heart.

The heart is an organ that pumps the blood through our bodies. Everyone knows that, but did you know that it is also a place where we store our inner most secrets and fears. It is our little hidey - hole where we bury our emotions, our most secret desires. So is it any wonder that we can feel these emotions through the heart itself. It is the very essence of our being, the core to our physical existence. Without the heart we cease to exist on the physical plane.

The heart is the one true place of the body that is sacred. It cannot be interfered with, tampered with. It will always stay true unto itself. It will put up a barrier, a shield to protect itself in times of great stress and sadness. Then as time goes past and the wound heals, the barrier comes down little by little until at last it is open once more to new and uplifting experiences. The hurt or sadness is still there, recorded for life in our memory banks, but it can no longer touch us. We have overcome it, grown from it. That is why after a great crisis in our lives, we are a much stronger person. The Soul, the heart essence was able to reach through the barrier that was placed around the heart to protect us from the surge of overpowering emotion. It is like an electrical current passing through our bodies. Without protection we could lose our way. Lose our grip on reality, our own reality. For we create our reality moment by moment, step by step, from one instant to the next. It is like building with building blocks, you can do and create whatever you choose too. There is a plan, a town plan you may call it. But these are only guidelines, there are no strict rules, no deadlines. The path will eventually lead you to the right destination. You can choose whatever path you wish to follow. You can take the short cut or you can choose the long scenic route with all the potholes along the way. You can stop and camp at any of these destinations for as long as you like until the urge to move on catches up with you. Until you feel deep within that there is something else waiting for you just over the horizon out of your view.

Whichever way you chose to walk, whatever building blocks you chose to build with, the outcome will be the same. Does this surprise you? Or does it stir up a distant memory of lives gone by when we have done just that very thing? Ended up right where we knew in our heart of hearts, we were meant to be.

CHAPTER EIGHT

Walking our path

Now let us move on to walking our path. It is very easy to sometimes lose our way in this physical life. We get so caught up in the energy that surrounds us. That intrudes in our own space. We sometimes without knowing it, mistake the energy we are picking up from someone close to us as our own

That is why it is important to continually white light ourselves, cleanse our aura, get rid of other people's energy before it overshadows our own. Make no mistake it can and will do this. It will overshadow us so completely that we can no longer distinguish what our own feelings are. We are left in a state of confusion, a state of despair and of course, we have no idea why we feel this way, or how to change it. Some people find themselves on a course of antidepressant drugs. This in turn renders them more helpless to the power of the other person.

So on it goes, we become more and more that other person, making no real decisions. Having or desiring not to have any say in the path we are walking. Leaving it up to someone else to walk our path for us. Do you see what I am leading to? If we allow someone else to take total control of our lives, we are missing it all together. We are losing the opportunity to build, to create. We are in actual fact hiding out in someone else's world. This way we cannot be blamed for someone else's mistakes, for we had nothing to do with it. It was not our fault. Once again fear is rearing its ugly head. Fear of failure, if we are not in control we cannot be to blame, to be made accountable for our mistakes. If we do not do anything we cannot fail. True?

By doing this, by allowing someone else to overshadow us, we are not being true to ourselves. We are living a lie. We can only do this for so long then the Universe will kick us where it hurts to wake us up. To make us take a good look at ourselves and what we are doing with our life. This life is a gift that we should use to the fullest.

This kick may come in the form of sickness, an accident or maybe even a break in the relationship that we have become so dependent on. Sometimes even then we are too afraid to let go, to walk our own pathway. Little by little, bit by bit, we are bought back to being able to create our own reality once more. But it can be a very slow process and some never really make it. They always hold back just that little bit. The fear of failure never leaves them. They lose themselves in space, they try to hide from the truth with drugs and alcohol. They find this easier than believing in themselves, then believing that they can do or be anything they desire to be.

So remember to white light yourself every night and morning. Also after a meeting with someone who left you feeling drained of all your reserves of energy. Imagine yourself in a tunnel of white light. See it pouring in from both ends completely immersing yourself in it. Ask to be cleansed and freed of any negative energy that has been trapped in your aura. Then once you have been cleansed, ask to be healed of any imperfections, any flaws or damage that has been done to your aura. Next, ask for a protective coating to be placed over the aura. So that anything other than that of the highest good, of the higher self just bounces off and goes back to where it came from with love.

CHAPTER NINE

Dancing to your own drum

Now let us talk about dancing to your beat, your own drum. Each and every one of us have a certain vibration we beat to. It is like a vibration rising up from within us calling to us. It is like a drum that serenades us. A song that uplifts us, carries our thoughts to other destinations, other galaxies to become part of a pool of thought. Group thought.

All thought rises up from within creating, absorbing our rhythm, our own beat then it rises to become part of the whole. So listen to your body, your movement, get a feel for your own balance. For this beat controls balance between body, mind and soul. It pulsates through you giving balance and harmony, do you not see? It is a throbbing pulsating beat that rises up from within the body calling out to the soul, with the mind. Look at me I am beautiful, I am magic, I am love.

It is a song of the heart truly rising up to embrace us, to surround us with love. It rises up like a yearning inside of us. An elation we feel when we know in our heart of hearts that we have connected, that we have balance with body, mind and soul. Even if it lasts only an instant the feeling is divine. It is so uplifting, so exhilarating, we know deep within that we have had a truly magical experience.

It is like discovering the universal song. For we all sing the same song, we just sing it to our own beat, hum to our own tune, vibrate to our own vibration. A truly magical experience is to listen to the whales' song for they are completely at one with the universe. They know all, they feel all, they experience all through their song of the universe. Listen, breath it in, experience it for yourself.

Once we have discovered our own song, our own beat, our own vibrational level, then there is no stopping us. The sky is the limit as you say. The magical feeling of elation will stay with us and we will simply glow. We will radiate so much power, so much energy for we will be in perfect harmony with the universe. Mother Earth, our soul. Is that not beautiful? Is that not a thing to strive for? Words cannot express the feeling of elation that comes with dancing to your own beat. You can feel it surging through you, within you. The blood in your veins pulsates it through every organ, gland and body part. The very essence of your being is pulsating to this beat and the feeling is immeasurable. It is divine. Once you reach this, you can tap directly into universal energy. You will feel it surging through your body in little bursts when it is needed.

This is really a state to aim for, the ultimate destination. Dancing to the beat of your own drum is putting yourself in a state of divine bliss where you feel the peace, the calm wash over you. Nothing phases you. You are at peace with yourself for you truly love yourself. You are at one with the universe.

Valerie Edwards

I want to be
Free, free, free
To let my Soul
Fly higher
Free, free, free
To let go of
All disguises

I want be able
To strip myself bare
Of all the illusions
All despair
I want to walk
In the sunshine
Leave the shadows behind

Dance to a tune
That is mine
Only mine
Wrap myself in colours
Vibrate with the drum

I want to
Merge with the wind
Dance with the rain
Soar with the Eagles
Feel my strength again
Feel the power
That is divine
Free to have
An open mind
To face the truth
Time after time
To love myself
For who I am

I want to shout
From the rooftops
Tell all the stars
That I have been
To Neptune and Mars
To galaxies beyond the sun
For I am God
Deep down inside
The truth from me
I can no longer hide
I can't escape
I no longer try
I want to be free
To let my thoughts fly

I want to be free
Free, free, free
To let my Soul
Fly higher
Free, free, free
To let go
Of all disguises

Free to experience
To love to grow
To wash in the beauty
Of this sacred rose
A flower so precious
So gentle so pure
How could you not
Just simply adore
You, yes you

CHAPTER TEN

Conclusion

I hope this book has been of some help in discovering the inner you. Do not get disheartened just keep plodding on, because believe me the rewards you reap from the journey will be enormous. You will fly beyond your wildest dreams. You will indeed soar with the Eagles. You will feel the love of self overwhelm you and the peace and contentment will be divine.

But you must stick to the guidelines and remember that you will only get out of it what you are prepared to put into it. It will take time and dedication. It will be easier if you relax and think of it as a great adventure you are going on. Enjoy it, have fun with it, do not be too serious. But most importantly, be honest for the only person you will be deceiving is yourself. If you are not honest with yourself, it will be a complete waste of time.

Remember the aim is to get a complete balance of body, mind and soul. There is no rush, it is not a competition. The only one judging you is yourself. You may take a lifetime to perfect this but what a journey you will have. Your life will be enriched in many ways, even if you never learn the universal song, the search itself will take you to many wondrous places. Enlighten you too many new truths.

You are truly loved by Spirit and we your Guides on this journey of discovery are on a pathway of our own. We also are experiencing many new truths, facing new challenges along our journey of enlightenment. We all have a pathway to follow, lessons to learn, we need to grow and develop just the same as you, only we have reached another level. We are doing it from another plane of existence. Just because your eyes cannot see us, this does not mean we do not exist. There are many things you cannot see with your physical eyes but when you have developed enough you will be able to see with your psychic eye. You may call it your third eye. So do not be alarmed when it happens, it will be a very gradual experience. It very rarely happens instantly. We do not work this way, we try to do everything very gently, very slowly little by little. We give you little gifts. Gifts of appreciation for all your dedication, for it really does take dedication and courage. Courage to stand up and be counted. To hold your head high and say, yes, I believe in spirit. I believe in life after death. I believe in my Guides, my teachers. This does indeed take much courage, much love of Spirit. But believe me you will be very well rewarded for this courage and dedication in so many ways. But remember, it all takes time, do not expect overnight results for you will be disappointed.

There are so many things you need to work through. So many truths you need to face. You need to be both spiritually and emotionally strong to do the work required of you. It will happen my dear ones, it will happen if this is what you truly desire deep within your heart. If you feel you are ready for the path ahead of you, we will help you. This little book is my gift to you, as to whether you follow it or not, the choice is yours and yours alone.

I love, I love
I love myself
With a love
That is burning stronger
It is rising up
In tidal waves
The current ever stronger
Washing over me in waves
Of emotion overwhelming
The more I learn
To love myself
The clearer is the picture
For love is truth
Yes honesty
In all its mighty glory
Will light the path
Will lead the way
Like crystal mountain waters
So pure, so sweet
So soft, so sure
Of the path
That they are taking
They never stray
Or lose their way
They trickle
Down the mountain

A surging force
They chart a course
To end up in the ocean
To merge as one
Beneath the sun
The salt and crystal waters
A gentle mass

That looks like glass
Or crashing waves like thunder
Now we are like
This mountain stream
Except we are thought
Not water
We wander along
Singing our song
Of joy, of pain, of sorrow
We create, we explore
Temptations galore
Can lead us from the mountain
We can lose our way
In the Earth's decay
Of smog, of greed, of famine
But we have a compass
Deep in our heart
A map that we can follow
To show us the way
A golden ray
Of hope that lives eternal
It pushes us on
With a gentle force
To lead us down the mountain

This force is love
Pure sweet love
A power ever stronger
It glows in the dark
We create in our heart
When fear just overwhelms us
It flickers on and off when doubt
Leaves us cringing in the corner
Hope is there to rescue us

We just have to listen
To the little voice inside our hearts
We call intuition
It is buried there
Beneath despair
We just have to find it

It is love you see
That is calling us
Love for all creation
It is surging up in gentle waves
Trying to awaken
The sleeping giant
With all its might
Buried deep within us
The power of one
The gentle son
That God sent to guide us
To set us free
To find the key
To unlock the love inside us
For we are one with the Universe
The stars, the sun, the planets
We ebb and flow
With the moons sweet glow
Surging through our pulses
The blood that runs
Through our veins
Is connected to the oceans
Pulsating at a gentle rate
That connects us
To Mother Nature

We all are one
The moon, the sun
Every living creature
The rocks, the trees
The gentle breeze
The grass, the Earth beneath us
Each playing a part
In this huge play
Going on around us
If we want a starring role
We must come up with answers
To rid ourselves
Of greed, of fear
Of ego's softly humming
Of doubt that overshadows faith
Keeping us from our path
Down the mountain
We have to learn
To love ourselves
If we are to find the way
To be a star
In this production of life
There is no other way.

Love and light to all who read my words

Your friend in Spirit

Red Eagle

Printed in the United States
By Bookmasters